THE CROSS

Its True Meaning

by

David Boyd Long

JOHN RITCHIE
CHRISTIAN PUBLICATIONS

John Ritchie
40 Beansburn, Kilmarnock, Scotland

THE CROSS

Its True Meaning

ISBN 0-946351-45-7

Copyright © 1994 by John Ritchie Ltd.
40 Beansburn, Kilmarnock, Scotland

Reprinted 1997

Typeset by EM-DEE Productions, Glasgow
Printed by Bell & Bain, Glasgow

Contents

Foreword

The material presented in this humble study has been burning in my mind and heart for years.

Book after book has been bought, borrowed, and perused in the hope that some able writer would really get to the real meaning of the doctrine of THE CROSS. It may be that there are such books but if so I have not found them or they do not appear to be in wide circulation. It was disappointing that no one seemed to get much beyond treating it as a synonym for the atoning work of our Lord.

Abler minds and pens than mine could have done a better job, but until they appear it is this writer's prayer that some hearts may be touched and some lives changed by the careful study of the subject and the Scriptures quoted.

It only remains to thank my patient friend Mr Tom Wilson of Glasgow who has several times gone through the "raw material" and with sharp eye and pruning knife, as well as many helpful and positive suggestions, has made it what it is.

I alone am responsible for whatever weaknesses and blemishes there may be.

David Long
Ballygowan, 6 May 1994

CHAPTER 1

Its True Meaning

AMONG evangelical Christians to-day this Biblical term, the cross, seems to be either poorly understood or else completely misunderstood. Whether our hymnology is the cause of this or the result of it is an open question, but we would be wise in any case to take our theology from our Bibles rather than from our hymnbooks. Clinging to "the old rugged cross to exchange it one day for a crown" or worse still "Carry your cross with a smile" may have emotional appeal and sentimental impact, but not one of the ideas will be found in Scripture. Neither do they come close to touching its true meaning. In the sense of the second quotation almost any unpleasant occurrence or affliction is seen as "just another cross which one must bear", from a painful back to a disagreeable superior at work. It must be understood that whilst a bad back or a demanding boss may be a discipline from God or a persecution by man, none had any part in the doctrine of the cross.

It is also true that weighty volumes can be found, some of them issued recently and authored by very learned and esteemed men in which the real meaning of the cross has been ignored entirely. Much of this is because the cross is seen merely as a synonym for the sacrificial and substitutionary work of Christ but nothing more. It is the belief of the present writer that the Scriptures show it to be very much more.

When the Holy Spirit consistently uses a certain word for a specific concept we may be certain that He has good reason for so doing. To think that we may exchange one of these Bible terms for another just to suit our taste is a mistake into which even some Bible translators have fallen.

Most literary experts use synonyms for the sake of

variety or graceful style and such usage can in general be justified. In more exact sciences, however, great care must be exercised, and lawyers, engineers, architects, medical specialists and the like rarely, if ever, indulge in the use of synonyms for the sake of literary appeal. Their business is much too serious and their definitions too important to allow for such liberties.

There is no business so serious as that of the Bible student or expositor, since he is dealing with divine revelation conveyed, we are assured by God Himself, in *words* which the Holy Ghost teacheth. Since these words are chosen by the Holy Spirit to convey to us eternal and spiritual truth about God's person, His plans, and His will for us, it is important that we pay strict attention to the Spirit's precise and consistent use of words not only to communicate truth, but also to distinguish between one truth and another, or even to emphasise different aspects of the same truth.

Nowhere in Scripture is the Spirit's exactness in the choice of words more evident than in those used in referring to different aspects of the atoning work of our Lord. We find terms such as: His death, His suffering, His offering, His sacrifice, His blood, His passion, and His cross, as well, of course, as the verb forms connected with these. The particular word used in any reference should be carefully noted, since, as noted above, such words suggest that each one is intended to draw attention to an important meaning or emphasis.

To illustrate this we might, without dogmatism, suggest that the term,

1. "Death of Christ" when used in Scripture usually focuses our thoughts on,
   a. The *voluntary* aspect of His death: "He poured out His soul unto death" (Isa 53:12); "He became obedient unto death" (Phil 2:8).
   b. The *substitutionary* nature of His death: "Christ died

for our sins" (1 Cor 15:3); "Christ died for the ungodly... Christ died for us" (Rom 5:6,8).

c. The *Reasons* for and the *Results* and *Blessings* flowing from His death: "He died...that He might be Lord" (Rom 14:9); "We were reconciled to God by the death of His Son" (Rom 5:10); "Through death to present you holy... in His sight" (Col 1:22).

2. The *Slaying,* as in Acts 5:30 was not by God but emphasises the fact that it was an act of deliberate violence and murder by men.

3. *Hanging* (and crucifixion) in the same passage emphasise the dishonour and degradation of the one so treated; see Deut 21:22; Josh 8:19; 2 Sam 4:12.

4. *Offering* and *Sacrifice* always underscore the Godward side of what was done, since man had no part in this; "He offered Himself without spot to God" (Heb 9:14); "He put away sin by the sacrifice of Himself" (Heb 9:26).

5. *Passion* and *Suffering* (same word in the original text) are connected with the pain and anguish of body and spirit experienced.

6. The *Blood* is the evidence of a life laid down and poured out, and seems always to emphasise the value of the work as in the words "precious blood" (1 Peter 1:19); "blood of His own" (Acts 20:23 JND). It is also worth noticing that the blood speaks of its value and efficacy but only *as applied* so we find the blood applied to the doorposts, to the altar, to the people, to the priests and their garments, to the scapegoat on the Day of Atonement, and to the leper and the live bird turned loose on "the day of his cleansing". In other words the value and efficacy of the blood depend on its being applied.

The emphasis in "the cross", however, is distinct from all these: it is the symbol of man's total rejection of God's Christ. It is never said that God gave His Son a cross, though of course it was part of the eternal purposes that it should happen. Man gave Him a cross; God gave Him the highest place far above all heavens, the name that is above every name and the promise of the throne of the universe.

It was not the custom of the Jews to crucify their criminals; they stoned them to death. The Romans did not crucify their citizens or others of rank or repute; it was a death of shame reserved for rebellious slaves, leaders of insurrection, and the scum of society. The Jews could have stoned Him as they stoned His martyr Stephen but that would not have served their purpose. They wanted to have Him degraded by crucifixion in order to destroy for ever any thought of worth, and to ensure that He would never become an object of worship or faith. How very wrong they were has been proved by the ages from then until now. Even in eternity our glorious Lord will be the centre of all worship with the very marks of that crucifixion still upon Him.

To achieve this degradation man gave the Lord a cross with all its horrifying accompaniments before and during the execution. We must remember, however, that not one single thing which man did or was capable of doing to Him could remove one sin because man could not put one sin upon Him. Only God could do that, and all that God did in making "His soul an offering for sin", and all our Lord did in bearing our sin was done during the hours of darkness when no human hand touched Him; no human voice was raised against Him and when, as far as the record goes, there was no human activity of any sort. With man shut out by the darkness, and the Lord Jesus shut in by it, the awesome transaction took place when God "did make to meet upon Him the iniquity of us all".

There is no recorded word from either Father or Son

during the darkness for during that period the Son, having become the sin offering and as such "made sin", was forsaken by God; no recorded communication took place between them. Only when redemption was completed and sin was "put away" did the light begin to dawn and the Son at last speak: "My God, my God why hast thou forsaken me" as our English Bible has it. Newberry points out that the tense really is "why *didst* thou...", as indicating something already past; and the RV margin along with the literal translations of Marshall and Green agree. Communion was again restored so He at last speaks, and if anyone wonders that He who was omniscient should ask "Why?", surely it must not have been for Himself that He asked but rather for us, in order that we might have some measure of His suffering and anguish in that darkness when He endured all the wrath and judgment of a holy God against sin. After that awful cry comes the triumphant shout, "It is finished" or consummated; and finally, "Father, into thy hands I commend my spirit".

The disciples of our Lord, in obedience to His teaching immediately took the cross as the badge of discipleship. He had been rejected and nailed to a cross and it would now be the emblem of their identification with Him in that rejection and reproach. Were they right in this? It is our view that they were, for so had the Lord Himself taught them long before the event.

CHAPTER 2

The Doctrine of the Cross Expounded in the Gospels

"THE cross", referring to the actual historical crucifixion, occurs eleven times in the four Gospels. With these we are not particularly concerned in our study. We are seeking the teaching of Christ about the spiritual significance and application of it.

The teaching of our Lord regarding the meaning of the cross is recorded six times in the first three Gospels. These teachings were all by the Lord Himself, all before the event, and all addressed to His own people. None of this teaching is recorded in the Gospel written by John. Of the six passages in which the meaning and importance of the cross are spelled out, four are positive, showing that the acceptance of the badge of rejection is essential for discipleship. These passages are: Matt 16:24; Mark 8:34; 10:21; Luke 9:23. Two more, Matt 10:38 and Luke 14:27, are phrased in negative terms, warning of the cost but insisting that without the acceptance of the cross and all it meant there could be no true discipleship. For any understanding of the doctrine and its implications these passages must be considered before we follow it through to the Epistles.

Our Lord's teaching on the subject
(The positive passages).

Context is very important if we are to understand what is involved in any passage of Scripture. In Matt 10 Christ sent out His disciples with power to perform miracles and preach the gospel of His kingdom. In chs. 11 and 12 He Himself goes around all the villages performing the miracles which authenticated His claim to be the Messiah. His crowning miracle in 12:22 was to cast out one of Satan's demonic agents; the response of the nation's leaders was to attribute this power to Satan himself. Christ called this attribution the sin against the Holy Spirit for which there is no forgiveness. He also pointed out the obvious illogicality of saying that Satan would empower anyone to cast out his own workers. At the end of the chapter the Lord shows that thereafter earthly ties and relationships would be overridden by new relationships: His true family would be His disciples who would do the will of His Father in heaven. Clearly at this point Israel's rejection of her Messiah was a fact.

The break with Israel having been made by her deliberate rejection of her Messiah, the Lord in a clearly symbolic act "went out of the house...sat by the seaside...went into a ship and, pushing out a little in the lake... spoke many things to them in parables". These are the parables of the mystery of the Kingdom and show the development of the spiritual kingdom during the present age of grace and the absence of the King. The earthly Messianic kingdom they had rejected when they refused the Messiah Himself. These parables also show the tactics of Satan in trying to obstruct, corrupt, and in any way possible defeat the absent King's purposes. This theme continues through chs. 13-16 at which point we find the Lord asking what men say of Him and finally "But ye, whom do ye say that I am?" (Matt 16:15). This question brings out Peter's confession of Jesus as "the Christ (Messiah), the Son of the living God". The Lord declares this to be a divine revelation and goes on to say that on that confession He would build His *ekklesia* or called-out congregation against which all schemes and purposes of hell would never prevail.

Then the disciples were startled by the words, "From that time forth Jesus began to show unto His disciples,

how that He must go to Jerusalem, and suffer many things
of the elders and chief priests and scribes, and be killed,
and be raised again the third day". Horrified at the thought
of what, according to human reasoning, would mean the
destruction of all Christ had just promised, the same Peter
who had just borne such a divinely-inspired confession now
blurts out in fleshy emotionalism, "Be it far from thee, Lord;
this shall not be unto thee!" Christ brands this statement
as the voice of a hidden but malicious adversary, since all
that He was predicting and must be done at Jerusalem
would be the fulfilment of the divine plan of the ages. Any
attempt at hindering this must be from the adversary (the
meaning of the word "Satan"), whoever's lips may be
actually used.

It was at this point that our Lord gave His very first
teaching on discipleship and the true meaning of the cross
as its badge and emblem. If their Master, in order to fulfil
the divine plan must go to Jerusalem and the cross, then
there was no way His true followers could evade the same
in their total identification with Him and all that He
represented. It was not a matter of being saved, for that
they already were, but a matter of following Him in
discipleship and the high cost of such a course.

The teaching opens with the blunt statement, "If any
man will come after me, let him deny himself, and take up
his cross, and follow me". The words must be considered
carefully and the meaning of each noted. First, the
individuality is emphasised: "if any man". In Luke 14:25-27
where the same doctrine is in view, though as we shall see
from the negative aspect, we read: "Great multitudes went
out with him and he turned and said unto them: If any
man come to me and hate not his father, and mother, and
wife and children, and brethren and sisters, yea and his
own life also, he cannot be my disciple". This choice would
not be made by the multitudes, but must be made by the
individual - any man. We shall come to this passage later.

Second, we must also note the word "will". "Shall" would indicate a statement of future fact but the verb "will" speaks of determinate purpose and choice as, for example, in 1 Tim 6:9 of those determined to be rich.

To "will" speaks of a voluntary choice; it also implies determination thereafter. The young man in Mark 10:22 when he heard of the cross and the high price involved, had a choice to make and he made it. He went away in full possession of all his wealth, but he also went away sad. We have all something to learn from this. The choice involved is whether or not to "come after" Him, meaning to take the same path as He was taking. The cross is more than salvation, it is discipleship.

Third, there follow two sharp commands; according to authorities on Greek the first two verbs draw attention to action is to be done at once: deny self (say no to all one's own desires, plans, or ambitions); pick up one's cross at once. It is also pointed out that here the tense changes for the verb "follow", to the present tense which gives it the sense of continuity, or constancy (A.T. Robertson); he must keep on following. In Luke 9:23 it says he must "take up his cross daily", so surely the sense is that with a mind firmly made up he immediately snatches up a cross which he makes his own, and daily keeps on taking it up as he follows the Master.

There is no need to weary the reader going over similar material in each of the three Gospels so we shall merely touch on one or two points where slight differences appear in the recorded narrative. We are not speaking of so-called "errors" for we accept the sacred writings as God-breathed and therefore, as originally written, free from error. It is true, however, that the Holy Spirit in guiding the writers was pleased to be selective. This means that for his own purposes each writer chose and ordered the material as directed by the same Holy Spirit.

We have already pointed out that Luke says the cross

must be taken up daily while the others do not. Matthew and Mark say essentially "What shall it profit a man if he gain the whole world and lose his own soul?", whereas Luke gives the final words as "lose himself" but as we shall see presently there is no conflict here for in the original though the words used are not the same, the sense is. Luke also adds the words "or be cast away" with which we shall deal in its place.

In all three of the Synoptics we have, after this teaching the fact of the Lord's coming mentioned with consequential approval and reward or disapproval and loss of reward. In Matthew all are judged according to their works. In Mark and Luke those who are ashamed of their Lord and therefore do not take their place with Him in rejection and reproach, will see Him ashamed of them. So the whole matter of receiving the Master's approval, His "well done" and His reward, is set over against His disapproval, His being ashamed of us, with consequent loss of reward.

In all the related passages the Lord makes it clear that for Him the path of finishing the work given Him by the Father meant the complete surrender to the will of One who sent Him and the yielding up of Himself not to be served but to serve; not to get but to give; not to clutch to Himself what was rightfully His own but to "make Himself of no reputation"; not to evade the cross as Peter suggested but to accept it with all that it meant. He had earlier told them of course that the servant was not greater than his lord, nor the one sent than He who sent him. In following Him and walking with Him there can be no evading of the cross. To all who follow Him the cross stands for the abrupt termination of the self life in being crucified with Him.

Well known in Gospel preaching are verses which in their original context were not addressed to the unsaved at all: "What shall it profit a man if he shall gain the whole world and lose his own soul; or what shall a man give in exchange for his soul?" It should first be noted that the word for "soul" (*psuchē*) not only means one of the three parts of man as a tripartite being, it also means "life", frequently the personal life of the individual including the sum of desires, ambitions, and plans. W.E. Vine calls it, among other things, the seat of personality, and cites the reference of Luke 9:24 where the word is translated "own self". The clinching argument is, of course, that the same word is translated "life" in the previous two verses and in all of the passages with which we are dealing. There we read in slightly different order, "He that saveth his life (that is for himself) shall lose it, but he that loseth his life for my sake shall keep it (or save it, or have it)". We would humbly submit that there is no reason of any kind, either in grammar or logic, for translating the same word as "life" in Matt 16:25 and as "soul" in the very next verse. Both the RV and the RSV translate the word as "life" in both verses and in all passages we are studying; Darby gives it in a footnote. In the context it cannot be a question of losing the soul in hell because these men were the Lord's very own, and the rendering in Luke 9:24 as his "own (personal) life" which will be lost makes this clear. In the Luke 9:25 passage the term "...or be cast away" is an unfortunate rendering much used by those who do not accept the eternal security of the believer. "Cast away" is the same term as in other passages "suffer loss" (1 Cor 3:15; Matt 16:26) and the preceding words mean to be destroyed or ruined. The words are given by most reliable interpreters as "ruining (or destroying) himself or suffering loss" which is, of course, quite different from losing his eternal salvation. F.W. Grant's comment is "he who would grasp the present must lose the future. There is no middle path".

The meaning is more easily grasped when we realise that to each one of us God has given one redeemed life to use for the absent Master's glory. This life may be preserved for Him by yielding it to Him and following Him in His path of total selflessness, or it can be retained for one's

own personal ends and ambitions in which case it will be a
life lost for God and ruined so far as usefulness is concerned.
Many a believer's marred life bears witness to the truth of
these verses.

Our Lord's teaching on the subject
(The negative passages).

As already noted the two negative passages to be
considered are: Matt 10:38, "He that taketh not his cross
and followeth after me, is not worthy of me"; Luke 14:27,
"and whosoever doth not bear his cross, and come after
me, cannot be my disciple".

The first occurrence of a doctrine, theme or office often
gives significant insight into its purpose or meaning. "The
law of first mention", as it is often called, is important in
interpreting Scripture; as has been said, the key to any
Bible doctrine is often found near the door. The first of these
two passages is the also first time the doctrine is given by
our Lord though not in the same fulness which we have
found in ch.16 of the same Gospel. The matter of context is
again important.

The Lord is here sending out His twelve apostles with
the gospel of His kingdom which would be a very important
moment for them, and no doubt one full of excitement. But
the Master knows the path before them and He forewarns
them of its difficulties and dangers. After instructions as
to how they should proceed He makes it clear (v.14) that
some will not receive them or their message. In v.16 He
reminds them that in their mission they will be as
vulnerable as sheep among wolves. From v.17 He tells them
that they will be summoned before religious courts, be
flogged in synagogues, appear before secular governors and
heads of state and be called upon to defend themselves. In
v.21 the troubles come closer when brother will hand over
his brother for execution. Father will do the same to his

child children will take sides against their parents and be the means of their death. These things seemingly were to be done to those who would accept the message and become followers of Christ.

From v.22 the messengers themselves would be universally hated for His name's sake and they would have to flee from town to town in the face of fierce persecution, while in v.24 He reminds them that in effect they would simply be suffering as He had suffered and would suffer, for the disciple is not greater than his Master, nor the servant above his Lord. In v.26 they are not to fear because everything will be made clear one day and all the mysteries will be explained. They are also not to fear because He who cares for the sparrows, the most worthless of birds, would care for them and though they suffered in body none of this could touch the soul.

From v.34 they are told that the gospel would divide between those who accepted it and those who did not, and that this cleavage would carry through their very own families for in v.36 a man's foes would become those of his own family circle. Herein lies the greatest test of all: "He that loveth father or mother more than me is not worthy of me: and he that loveth son or daughter more than me is not worthy of me. And he that taketh not up his cross and followeth after me is not worthy of me". Nothing and no one is to take the place of Christ in the heart of the disciple, no matter how close. The word for "love" here is not the strong word *agapē* but *phileō* which is more like fondness or affection between friends or family members. We are being taught here that no ties of affection or fondness, even of family (and these surely are among the strongest ties known to man) are to be allowed to come between us and devotion to the Lord. Our Lord Himself experienced this for we are told that "even his brothers believed not on Him" and at the end of ch.12 of this Gospel He said that His family was made up of those who did the will of His Father in heaven.

Two things in this story will strike the careful reader as strange:

1. In 10:23 the Lord says that they shall not have gone over the cities of Israel, till the Son of man be come, yet when they had finished their mission and returned the Son of man had not come in any new or different way.

2 . Though we learn from the following chapters that while some believed many did not; some were in confusion and doubt; and some queried and even mocked, there is no record of the court and synagogue trials, floggings, betrayals by family members, and even the handing over of these to execution. Indeed later, when the seventy returned as recorded in Luke 10:17 they were rejoicing in the results of their missionary endeavours. From this we gather that what the Lord said was intended to cover the whole history of the faithful disciple bearing witness, and suffering for it, right until the Lord's return. The early preachers after Pentecost certainly faced violent opposition before the council of the Sanhedrin with beatings, threats, and imprisonment. As time went on this became more fierce with the murder of Stephen, the scattering of the believers, and the persecution of whole areas of local churches by Saul of Tarsus. Then, upon his conversion, he himself suffered "the loss of all things"; "was made a spectacle to men and angels". The narrative of his sufferings in the NT makes one wonder that anyone could survive it all. He was certainly hailed before councils, governors, and kings, was betrayed, imprisoned, and finally executed.

From then until now faithful witnesses for Christ have always suffered, and the roll-call of martyrs is long from the burnings and torments under the Caesars down through the ages to the Reformation times, and the Inquisition;

hardly a country in Europe has not been stained with blood, tears, and ashes even to Britain itself. True disciples will always bear the cross of rejection and suffering, and those who would escape it by turning away from such a high cost must accept the responsibility of facing the One who first bore the cross to show us the way, but will one day call us to account for every unfaithfulness.

In spite of the last two paragraphs there may still be some, strange though it seems, who feel that this teaching about taking up the cross is somehow not valid or applicable in our day. In the light of all this can it be maintained with any seriousness that there is some sort of basic difference between the Christians of the NT and those of to-day?

All those redeemed by Christ's death on the cross are one body, seen by God to have been crucified with Christ, raised together with Him and with each other, and seated together in the heavenlies in Christ. It seems strange that a basic doctrine like that of the cross should apply to one early section of the believers of the church age but not to another.

If such doubters (or quibblers?) there be, we would suggest a careful reading, for example, of 2 Corinthians. In that letter Paul gives us no less than six lists of the sufferings which he endured and was still enduring because he was a servant of Christ. If we believe in divine inspiration of Scripture we cannot construe this as mere boasting or self-pity on the part of the writer. Though the cross is not specifically named, its teaching quite obviously underlines the whole catalogue of suffering. In 4:7 he says "always bearing about in our bodies the dying of Jesus Christ", and again "always delivered to death for Jesus sake". In 6:4 he says "as dying we live", and in 11:23 we read "in deaths oft". But not only Paul, Peter has this to say, "As Christ hath suffered for us in the flesh, arm yourselves also with the same mind". John in Rev 1:9 refers to himself as "your brother and companion in tribulation, and in the kingdom and patience (endurance) of Jesus Christ".

We are thus forced to the conclusion that in the Gospels the emphasis is on "taking up the cross" because it was at that time a new teaching, while in the Epistles we have the practical application of that teaching to the believer's everyday life.

In the Lord's commissioning of His apostles in Matt 28 the first step is "go ye therefore and teach (make disciples) of all nations"– no distinctions. The next step is "baptising them...", symbolising the abrupt termination of the old life – no extensions. The last step is "teaching them to observe all things whatsoever I have commanded you", the beginning of the new life – no exemption.

It all applies to every believer in every phase or level of the life: public, home, marital, business, professional or financial. There are no exceptions and if anyone thinks this standard too high then we can only reply that the Bible expositor or teacher has no authority to set a lower one.

CHAPTER 3

The Doctrine of the Cross Expounded in the Epistles.

IT is an interesting fact that the doctrine of the cross is expounded in the NT Epistles by Paul alone and yet he, it should be remembered, is the only writer of Epistles who had not, it seems, heard the Lord while He taught on earth. Heb 12:2 may be seen by some as a possible exception to Paul's authorship. The term "the cross" is found eleven times in Paul's letters, while the verb form "to crucify" appears ten times in the same. It is also significant that all these were addressed to believers, and in almost every case not specifically connected with their salvation, but rather with their present way of life, attitude and behaviour.

In Rom 6:6 for example, we read "our old man is crucified with Christ". The great theme of Romans is God's grace in saving the sinner, but that grace can never be at the expense of His holiness. He cannot overlook or justify sin, so the sin was judged and put away in the person of a substitute. On that basis salvation is entirely of grace apart from human works, and all the believer's sins past, present, and future have been atoned for. This preaching of grace was a new concept and the Gentile believer might be inclined to take advantage of it by imagining that since all his sins and also his sinfulness (as to his nature) had been covered by the atonement he could live as he liked without fear. It is also possible that Paul was dealing with a supposed argument by an opponent of the doctrine of grace. Whatever view is taken it is a gross error, and the latter is the one most to be feared.

Since the repentant and believing sinner is seen by God to have died in the person of his substitute, and has confessed this symbolically in his baptism, how could he possibly justify any thought of living the old life of sin? This is why we link the doctrine of the cross with the individual life of the believer, and we shall be expanding this later.

In the Corinthian letters, the cross features greatly:

1 Cor 1:13	"Was Paul crucified for you?"
1 Cor 1:17	"Lest the cross of Christ be made of no effect"
1 Cor 1 :18	"The preaching of the cross is... foolishness"
1 Cor 1:23	"We preach Christ crucified"
1 Cor 2:2	"Nothing among you but Christ crucified"
1 Cor 2:8	"Had they known they would not have crucified"
2 Cor 13:4	"(Christ) was crucified through weakness"

In these letters, while individual living and holiness are undoubtedly involved, the whole context shows it to be in a framework of congregational responsibility. They are reminded that they are all members of a body, the body of Christ, and that each member of that body must interact responsibly and harmoniously with all other members. All ostentation and pride, all clashing by taking each other to secular courts, all conceited parading of giftedness, is the activity of the flesh and this flesh must be seen as having been nailed to the cross that no longer should it assert itself in the believer's life. Down to our day we must confess that the ugly head of flesh has still led to disorder, strife, and even to divisions as at Corinth: "I of Paul, and I of Appollos, and I of Cephas, and I of Christ" (1:12-13). Far more trouble has been caused among us by the activity of the flesh (or self, or carnality) than by serious differences regarding doctrine or practice.

The Galatians too had to face the challenge of cross teaching:
3:1   "Jesus Christ hath been set forth crucified..."

5:11 "Then is the offence of the cross ceased"
5:24 "They that are Christ's have crucified the flesh with its affections"
6:12 "Persecution because of the cross"
6:14 "Glorying only in the cross"

In Galatia it was, of course, a doctrinal problem but one which flowed from pride and self-aggrandisement rather than from heretical doctrine such as denial of the deity of Christ. It was a bending of the lines of distinction between law and grace. It must be confessed that among Christians to-day legalistic rigidity and harshness has caused many a hurt and brought about the ruination of the collective testimony of many a congregation. Indeed, every failure in the NT churches has been seen, and is being seen, around the globe down to our own day. Sin must be judged and dealt with, frictions must be settled but not in secular law courts, always within the local assembly, members of the body must work together in harmony and love under the direction of the divine Head. But if this is to be done then "the flesh" must be seen as having no place before God or in Christ. It must go to the cross.

Other epistles too avert the reader's gaze to the cross:

Eph 2:16 "Hath reconciled both in one body by the cross"
Phil 2:8 "Obedient... even (to) the death of the cross"
Phil 3:18 "Enemies of the cross"
Col 1:20 "Made peace by the blood of His cross"
Col 2:14 "The writing...against us nailed to the cross"
Heb 12:2 "He endured the cross despising the shame"

CHAPTER 4

The Cross in Corinthians

THIS letter was addressed to a worldly-wise and carnal congregation of immature (baby) Christians. They were full of pride and conceit in their gifts, abilities, knowledge, and accomplishments. They appear to have been puffed up by their intellectual emancipation (for example, glorying in the fact that they were being liberal with the incestuous adulterer of ch.5), yet weak and quarrelling, divided and defiled, disoriented in doctrine and disorderly in assembly practice. All the ugly characteristics of the old nature were being flaunted by a people who in God's eyes had been crucified with Christ. It is for this reason that the Holy Spirit through Paul introduces from the very first chapter the teaching of the cross as the cure for all their ills and problems.

The apostle reminds them that even when he came first to Corinth with the gospel he had chosen deliberately not to preach in the word-wisdom of men. Corinth had a country-wide reputation as imitators of the Greek intellectuals and philosophers each one of whom had his followers and from whom each little group proudly took its name and whose manners they aped – those of Socrates, Aristotle, Demonsthenes, and so on. They fancied themselves as dialectic debaters and, like their Athenian models were forever chasing after the latest philosophical novelty. Paul had just come from Athens where he had seen this spirit in full flower and it would almost seem as though he tried to adopt a style which might attract them for we are told in Acts 17:21, "all the Athenians and strangers which were there spent their time in nothing else, but either to tell, or to hear some new thing". Certainly the style he used there seems quite different from the record we have of other addresses of his. He may also have already met some Corinthians there among these strangers or at least he knew of them. At Athens the results seem to have been comparatively sparse.

"So Paul departed from them" and came straight to Corinth where he says that he was determined not even to give the appearance of catering to their fancied Grecian intellectualism. He would preach Christ and Him crucified and the stigma of that cross would neither be avoided nor minimised. He knew that a gospel based on the total setting aside of all that man is in himself, or can do for himself, would never be popular with the natural man apart from the enlightening work of the Holy Spirit. He was also aware that to preach such a gospel would be considered either madness or stupidity (1:18). Man wants to hear about his own potential, though he might accept a gospel which tells him that he needs a little help here and there, or a little orientation to enable him to unleash all his hidden abilities.

God blows on all of man's pretensions and continues to save when the gospel is proclaimed with "great plainness of speech" and without any of the ornamentation which is so dear to the heart of man. Our Lord made Himself a working Galilean and was despised for not belonging to the schools of His day. Their concept is clear in the words "How knoweth this man letters, having never learned?" (John 7:15). Everything He said was in the plainest and simplest of terms with no fancy terminology or jargon words of His time. Likewise His disciples were common working men who were referred to as "ignorant and unlearned". This did not mean that they were uncouth ignoramuses, to which idea their writings give the lie. It simply means that they were not the product of the elite schools. Paul was, of course a highly-educated man, but he is the one who said: "I determined to know nothing among you but Christ and Him *crucified* (1 Cor 2:2). It would seem that in our day we need to learn this lesson all over again, as Paul knew the Corinthians did.

The gospel of the cross tells man that he is by nature lost and ruined, for who but ruined and totally-evil man could have taken the Son of God and nailed Him to a cross after spitting in His face? It also tells that he is under the judgment of God, indeed judged and "condemned already". It tells him that if he is to find salvation he must be put to death in the person of his divine substitute so that by the operation of the Holy Spirit he can be born anew and thus made a child of God. The religious signs sought by the Jews and their followers, as well as the philosophical reasonings so admired by the Greeks and their mimics in all ages, would not be found in Paul's preaching of the cross which stumbles the one and outrages the other. Nevertheless, because it is the power of God unto salvation it brings men to new life since it begins by destroying the old life, something the philosophies, old or new, could never do.

But Paul goes farther back still for in 1:26 we see that not only the gospel, but their calling in the sovereign counsels of God, was connected with the cross and its nullifying effect on the flesh. It is the weak, the lowly, the poor, even those whom the world considers to be "nothing" who are chosen by God so that "no flesh should glory in His sight", though we know how precious in the sight of men are birth, power, wealth, social status, and the like. God must have all the glory so we see that in the cross man and all his pretensions are set aside in judgment. In the new life which he has found in Christ nothing should be seen of him or his standards. Thus, in the light of the doctrine of the cross, when the believer acts in the flesh or according to its principles he is flying in the face of all that the cross means, reversing all that God has planned, robbing Him of His glory, and of course making it impossible for Him to work spiritually through us. In our flesh "dwelleth no good thing" (Rom 7:18; see also 8:13). The reader should also read carefully Rom 6.

Every single error and disorder in the Corinthian

assembly we repeat, was the result of either not understanding the doctrine of the cross or of setting it aside. Their moral laxity, unruly arrogance, ostentatious parading of "their gifts", their over-readiness to be speaking in public gatherings, their brashness in propagating false doctrine regarding the resurrection (ch.15); all were manifestations of the flesh which was not seen as crucified, but was alive and active.

In ch.5 they were slow to judge sin, so open that it was common knowledge, and of such a nature as not be even mentioned in the pagan society around them. They were not mourning over such a disgrace but "puffed up" and "glorying", possibly preening themselves that they were liberated from any sort of old-fashioned puritanical narrowness, or perhaps that they were trying to "rehabilitate" graciously for further usefulness.

In ch.6 they were wrangling about matters of personal rights and self-interest and were not prepared in humility to seek God's solution or to submit their disagreements to the judgment of the overseers of the church. Instead they were prepared to accept the solution of the pagan courts, the very courts in which their Lord had been condemned to death, a bizarre and wrong-headed business, but such is the flesh when not dealt with at the cross. In the latter part of the same chapter they are sharply warned to "flee fornication" which probably means that they were to give a wide berth to all forms of sexual immorality, a gross expression of the activity of the flesh.

In chs. 12 and 14 their pride and glorying in their gifts is rebuked as being nothing but the flesh, and that flesh God sees as crucified. The more we read of the Corinthian letter the clearer it becomes that the cross and all it meant was being ignored. The flesh still ruled. They were indeed "carnal" or "walking after the flesh", though it is to be noted that the believer is "not *in* the flesh" (Rom 8:9) though he may allow it to intrude *into* his life.

It is very easy to see and condemn such carnality and its results in a congregation so far from us in time and culture. It would, however, be either blindness or hypocrisy on our part to deny that in our own day as much damage has been done to ourselves and the church's testimony by the same activity of the flesh.

Has there not been lack of comprehension as to God-given gifts, the abuse of such gifts or the ignoring of the whole teaching regarding them and their use? Have we not often seen the whole question of gift by-passed to give everyone, gifted or not, his turn on the platform? It is also not unknown for unspiritual men to be in positions of oversight and authority for which they are unqualified, yet from which there is insufficient spiritual power to remove them. We have little right to criticise those at Corinth.

The God of order teaches us that all things are to be done decently and in order, yet the gatherings have often been marred by indecent disorder of one sort or another. In some gatherings the divine instruction as to the godly woman's deportment, function, and head covering are set aside to bring us more into line with modern trends.

It is interesting to recall that the practice of women covering their heads was carefully observed by all mainline denominations both Roman and Reformed throughout the centuries without dissent or resistance until the Woman's Liberation Movement burst on the scene in the world.

Would it be going too far to suggest that the trend to more and more entertainment in the form of musical programmes usurping the time and place of serious Bible teaching is often little more than a catering to the flesh? From a slightly different angle W.W. Fereday commented more than half a lifetime ago that "mere addresses, carefully planned, with points, divisions, anecdotes, and alliterations may be entertaining but it is doubtful if they instruct or reach hearts and consciences about evils from which the hearers should purge themselves". Harold St.

John referring to "the instructed scribe" in Matt 13:52 has pointed out (*Collected Writings* vol. 2 pp. 22,23) that in this age of the King's absence "the outstanding mark of a christian assembly is that it is a place where the Scriptures are expounded... it is a place where the Scriptures are interpreted as God gave them, that is by the chapters, books, and sections, not in text preaching, though I do not object to that... Elders... brethren, I beseech you be exercised and see to it that you feed the flock of God. And so we repeat, the Lord expects that my assembly will be a place for the exposition of the Word". In many places to-day however, there is little appetite for expositional teaching because tastes have been developed for the lighter fare of little encapsulated in messages or sermons. This is a situation which reminds one of the Hebrew believers who are chided by the writer with the words "when for the time ye ought to be teachers, ye have need that one teach you again what the first principles (the ABCs) of the oracles of God; and are become such as have need of milk, and not strong meat (food). For every one that useth milk is unskilful in the word of righteousness; for he is a babe". In the next verse he gives a hint as to the reason for their spiritually infantile condition when he writes. "But strong meat (food) belongeth to them that are of full age, even those who by reason of use have their senses exercised to discern both good and evil". In other words constant dependence of spiritual baby food robs one of the appetite for adult nourishment, and by the same token disciplining oneself in serious spiritual nourishment develops a growing appetite for it. A child allowed to indulge itself habitually in crisps, chips, chocolates, sweets and coke loses all desire for decent nourishing food. It is a living parable.

In the two Corinthian letters the word "edifying" or upbuilding is used some fifteen times as verb or noun showing the importance of it in light of their problems. They abounded in utterance and knowledge and came behind in no gift yet they were tearing themselves apart in sectarian strife.

We would not have far to look in our own day to see the same spirit and its results. In Eph 4:11 we find that all gift from the ascended Lord are "for the perfecting of the saints... for the edifying of the body of Christ till we all come to the unity of the faith..." Almost every objective given here was being nullified by the formation of little groups and circles around favourite teachers. Dare we affirm that we are free from this to-day? Should we not bow out heads as we see the ruination of testimony and the grieving of many hearts caused by this? True gifting from God can be used for leading us to "the unity of the faith" or perverted to the forming of sectarian circles, and the latter is certainly the product of the flesh.

The word of God is clear in the command of Rom 6:17,18, "Mark them which cause divisions and offences contrary to the doctrine which ye have learned, and avoid them. For they that are such serve not our Lord Jesus Christ".

CHAPTER 5

The Cross in Galatians

IN Galatians the cross is mentioned in three passages, and again the basic subject is connected with giving the flesh place, though here it is in an individual and theological context rather than a behavioural setting.

The Jewish legalists were insisting that Gentile believers, which most of the Galatian believers were, must submit to circumcision and observe the ceremonial law with the feasts and holy days as well as the dietary regulations. Paul argues, by the Holy Spirit of course, that this would put them squarely back under the law, which he says in 6:12 would be "making a fair show in the flesh" which should have been seen as crucified. This would be saying in effect that they judged themselves capable of keeping that law. Paul had already said that the believer is "dead to the law" (2:19), that is as having been crucified with Christ, whereas they would be resurrecting one dead in God's sight and putting him under a legal system which he also says "neither we nor our fathers were able to bear". It is the old theme of getting back to activity in the flesh instead of reckoning it dead through the cross.

On the one hand they would be used as trophies of Judaistic missionary zeal; on the other they would be doing something to add to their salvation, and in circumcision they would be wearing the proud badge of the Jewish covenant in which in reality they had no part. From whatever angle we view this it can only be seen as the pride of the flesh. They would be saying, in effect, that man was not totally lost and incapable of doing something to save himself. By conforming in this way they might also escape the contempt of the Jews and be accepted by them as inside the Judaistic fold.

In that latter connection Paul says in 5:11 that the offence or stumbling block of the cross might have been avoided had he preached a legalistic ritualism which caters for man's pride by giving him something which he can do and take pride in. In 6:2 he says that persecution by the Jews might also be side-stepped in the same way. It is all, so the legalist's argument goes, a matter of giving man some little reason for glorying, some little loophole for his pride, the tiniest little face-saver which would make his position just a little more acceptable to him and to those around him. But God will have none of it. Salvation must be by grace or not at all. All have sinned; all stand guilty before God; none can do anything to save himself; every mouth is stopped. Man must acknowledge that "in his flesh dwelleth no good thing". He has to see that the judgment pronounced on him has been executed on the person of his substitute and that judicially in God's reckoning he himself has died with, and in, that substitute. Thus he can stand before God justified in Christ. In all of this the flesh has no place, for old things have passed away and all things have become new. As redeemed, man's only glory is in the cross by which he died out from under the curse of a broken law and therefore he dare not put himself back under it again.

This is why in the third passage (6:14) Paul in effect says that he will glory in nothing but the cross which entirely rules out his wretched self and all that pertains to self. In other words He is glorying in the judicial death and removal of the sinful "old man" of whom he is now ashamed and with whom he wants nothing to do.

And what will this mean in terms of his relationship with the world, including the apostate religious world? The effect of the application of the cross is that from the moment when it is genuinely and intelligently accepted, it puts me in the place of death so far as the world in all its aspects is concerned, and puts the world in the place of death so far as I am concerned. We emphasise "the apostate religious world" because the great mainline so-called church structures are, in the main a total departure from the NT simplicity which have developed into a wealthy, complex, politically-oriented, organisation where the most ungodly can feel comfortable and are urged to join.

When the world – civil, social, political, and religious – drove our Lord outside its gates and "slew Him, hanging Him on a tree (the cross)", it judged itself and sealed its own doom. It is also true that when Christ's disciple takes up that cross and associates himself with this rejected Master there is really no place for him in the world except the place of the pilgrim and the stranger on his way to a better country. He sees himself associated with Christ going out to Skull Hill bearing a cross while the elite of the world mock him for his folly. All this is summed up in the phrase "the reproach of the cross".

We, of course would hardly be tempted to insist that Gentile believers be circumcised and keep all the feast days and commandments of the Mosaic code. Yet we can allow a harsh and unlovely spirit of narrow legalism to blight our attitudes toward our brethren. We are instructed by Scripture to be strict and severe in self-judgment and examination of our own hearts and ways, but we are also reminded that we should not "judge another man's servant", meaning of course the Lord's servant which every brother is. We are also reminded sharply that if we have been doing this we are to desist forthwith; "Let us not, therefore, judge one another *any more*".

When I sit in judgment on my brother for what I think he should do nor not do, I am attempting to usurp the place of his divine Master.

CHAPTER 6

The Cross in Hebrews

IN Heb 12:2 Christ is held up before the believer as the prince, leader and model of His people who are urged to keep "looking off" to Him "who endured the cross despising the shame and is sat down on the right hand of the throne of God". This is said because they were a sorely-tried and confused people in danger of "becoming weary and fainting in (their) minds" (v.3). They too were in a race; a gruelling reliability trial in the same world in which their fore-runner had "finished the work" which the Father had given Him to do. The above words draw to a close a section which began as far back as 10:32, ch. 11 being parenthetical.

In that inspired diversion (ch. 11) we are given a parade of witnesses or testimony bearers, men and women who had run the same race which we are called to run, had lived the life of faith and finished their course, as our examples. The writer of our epistle reminds his readers at the end of ch.10 that they too had started off well, "enduring a great fight of affliction". Then comes a list of words describing what they had endured: becoming a gazing stock, reproaches, afflictions, being companions of others who were so treated, taking joyfully the plundering of their belongings. Then comes the challenge: "The just shall live by faith (that is not looking to the material, the physical, or on self)... but if he draw back my soul does not take pleasure in him" (JND). The drawing or shrinking back is from the high cost of following a rejected leader and the illustration in terms of Israel's history has already been brought forward more than once in this epistle. The shrinking back at Kadesh Barnea was when they rebelled and preferred to go back into the wilderness rather than face the battles of the land. God was not then pleased with those who shrank back, nor is He now with the same kind of behaviour by those professing to be disciples.

God's ancient people had been saved from death by the blood of the lamb, redeemed from Egyptian slavery by divine power, committed to the God-given leader in the cloud and in the sea, and at Sinai brought into covenant relationship with God, again by blood. They went on well but a series of failures left them weakened and when at Kadesh Barnea the voice of the majority frightened them with tales of the high price for the conquest of the land they shrank back from leaders Joshua and Moses (both of whom picture Christ), and went back to "ruination and loss" in the parallel of the Gospels we have been studying. In 10:35 now the first-century Hebrew Christians are urged not to cast away their confidence which had great reward. It was reward they were in danger of losing, not their eternal life. We did see that in each of the three Gospels Christ's teaching wound up with reward won or lost. We must keep in mind that Canaan, many of our hymns notwithstanding, is not a picture of heaven but of the enjoyment of our spiritual blessings in the heavenlies. They had to fight for every foot of Canaan for there were daunting enemies there; when we read in Ephesians that all our blessings are in the heavenlies we are also told that we need armoured and courageous battling to retain the enjoyment of those blessings since we have ranged against us "principalities... powers, rulers (cosmocrats) of the darkness of this age, spiritual wickednesses in the heavenlies" (Eph 6:12).

At this point comes the assurance: "but we are not of them who draw back to perdition, but of those who have faith to the saving of the soul" (10:39). The word "perdition" almost automatically turns most minds to hell and the lake of fire but W.E. Vine points out that it is the word used for the "marred wineskins" in Luke 5:37. These were not necessarily thrown into the fire, and may well have been used for other purposes such as patching a sandal. They certainly were ruined or destroyed for their original purpose as was the life "ruined" according to Christ's teaching of the cross. It is also interesting to note that the word for the saving of the "soul" here in Hebrews is the word we have studied in all three Gospels for the saving of one's personal "life" for God and His purposes.

These are very solemn passages which call for careful and unbiased study. It is so easy to apply them to those who were never saved, which of course makes it more comfortable for us.

It may be asked what bearing this history of God's people has on Christians of the twentieth century. It happened over three thousand years ago to people of a different race travelling through a wilderness, so what can it mean to us? The answer is to be found in 1 Cor 10:6-11, and it must be remembered that the majority of those were obviously Gentile Christians living in a bustling Greek city. Yet the writer says in these verses that all that happened to the Israelites was to be taken by the Corinthians as examples that they should not fall into the mistakes of which the Israelites were guilty (v.6). In v. 11 he goes further and states categorically that not only did these things happen as examples to them, but that the whole experience was actually recorded "for our admonition (warning) on whom the ends of the world (ages RV, JND) are come". This last phrase means that the recorded example and warning are applicable to us right to the end of time.

Heb 3:8-11 is a quotation from Ps 95 which tells us that it refers to the "forty years in the wilderness". We know that the words "I sware in my wrath that they should not enter into my rest" are taken from Num.14 where their failure was in refusing to go forward into the land of promise because the cost was too high. There are two further references to this same incident and they are all held up as warnings to these suffering and confused Jewish Christians who were being tempted to "go back" to the temple and its ceremonies. Hence the challenging cry at the end of ch.10, "But we are not of those who draw back to perdition (ruination or destruction), but of them who believe to the saving of the soul". A closer translation of the last phrase would be "but of them who have faith (it is a noun and not a verb) unto the preserving of the life" that is for God.

These quotations are an obvious reference to the turning or shrinking back at Kadesh Barnea, and the link with the cross is obvious when we put the words quoted alongside those of the Lord's teaching on the cross in the Synoptic Gospels. There we saw that one may shrink back from the cross as the emblem of discipleship, thus saving the life for self. In so doing, however, his life becomes a loss so far as God's purposes are concerned. God did not redeem His ancient people to leave them in Egypt serving Pharaoh, nor to become little grave mounds in the sand of the desert. No more does He save us from the old life so that we might have a better time in the world from which He has just taken us for Himself.

The story of Paul's conversion is recorded three times in Acts; once by Luke and then twice directly from the mouth of Paul himself. In none of these accounts is it said that his salvation was from hell or for heaven though of course that was included. In the first case God said to Ananias, "he is a chosen vessel unto to me to bear my name unto the Gentiles".

In his defence before Agrippa he said that God had spoken to him in the temple and had told him that he was chosen to be a witness and to open the eyes of those in darkness and he added, "Whereupon, O king Agrippa I was not disobedient to the heavenly vision". He knew that a work had been given him and that to do other than to accept it would be disobedience. We need more and more to realise that we have been saved by God for a purpose, and that to fail to fulfil that purpose is to disobey God to the spoiling of our redeemed lives.

CHAPTER 7

The Cross in Ephesians.

IN Eph 2:16 we have a startling application of the doctrine of the cross. It is also a very humbling one if properly understood. The Holy Spirit, through the apostle Paul, has been showing the Ephesian Christians all the limitless blessings which are theirs as in the heavenlies in Christ Jesus. In 2:13 he reminds them of how degraded their condition was before conversion. In plain language he summarises this as "the lusts of the flesh"; and "the desires (will or demands) of the flesh and of the mind". They were also seen as "dead in trespasses and in sins". He then adds in v.12 that they were without Christ (the Messiah) and therefore aliens with no covenantal claim on God, and so, without hope.

He had earlier stated that they had been quickened or brought to life together with Christ which takes for granted that they had already died with Him. Not only that but they had been seated together in the heavenlies in Christ. We are said to be there "*in* Christ" so the "together" has to mean together with all other saints, both Jew and Gentile.

In v.13 the far-off Gentiles are made near by the blood of Christ because He is our peace (note the Jewish writer's use of "our" again) who has broken down the dividing wall and made both Jew and Gentile one. If we are careful readers, this statement should stop us in our tracks. Hebrew and pagan; Jew and Gentile sitting together in peace, oneness, and blessing! How could this ever be? Even Peter said in Acts 10:28, "Ye know how that it is an unlawful thing for a man that is a Jew to company, or to come in unto one of another nation". Centuries, yea millennia, of antagonism and hatred from the conquest of Canaan and the extermination of its inhabitants, had built a wall between Jew and Gentile. The law of God had also legislated against any kind of mixture or intercourse. To this barrier would be added pogroms, persecutions, jealousies, suspicions, to which we must add the later fires of the Inquisition; originally instituted against Jews; and of Hitler's camps and gas chambers. All would form a wall that no human power could surmount or remove. How does God propose to break down the wall, abolish the enmity, making of the two one new man (2:14,15)?

In spite of all man's vaunted wisdom, and his clever schemes and programmes, his leagues, blocks, and diplomatic approaches, he has never succeeded in doing this, and never will. How helpless they are in the face of the paranoiac hatred between Jew and Arab today! The latter demands nothing less than the driving of the Israeli nation into the sea, while the former has no intention of being driven anywhere. Yet God has done what man cannot do and is still doing it by "(reconciling) both unto God in one body by the cross having slain the enmity thereby", that is by the cross (2:16). The only way they could ever be reconciled was by putting both Jew and Gentile to death by the cross of their substitute, and then raising them to a new life in Christ "where there is neither Greek nor Jew, circumcision nor uncircumcision, Barbarian, Scythian, bond or free: but Christ is all and in all" (Col 3:11). That is Christ is everything and in everyone and in Him no one is seen as anything but a Christian.

This was beautifully illustrated to the writer many years ago at a Bible conference in North America. During the break between sessions I was standing with a couple of men chatting about the Jewish/Arab question in the light of prophecy. I had just referred to the bitter hatred which both have to Christ when a handsome young couple came up arm-in-arm. I stopped in mid-sentence not wishing to give offence. The young lady smiled in understanding, as she had obviously overheard a snatch of the conversation, and then introduced themselves saying; "I am Rahel and this is Achmed my husband. I am a Jew and he is an Arab but we have solved the Arab/Jewish problem in Christ". She went on to say, however, that they had both been put out of their homes and disinherited by their families, forbidden the use of the family names; in her case her family had celebrated her funeral and now considered her legally dead. The concept of "the cross" had become very real to them. Something different from, and beyond, a synonym for Christ's atoning death by which they had been saved. It was now the badge of their identification with a scorned and hated Christ. It was in truth the reproach of the cross. Would to God it were as real to every believer!

The natural feelings of race, nationality, culture, even social or economic position die hard, even in the believer. The directors of a deeply-spiritual missionary society in China have recorded their shock at finding, in World War 1, that it became necessary to move to separate stations fellow missionaries of British and German backgrounds. Their General Secretary said that nationalistic prejudices seemed to be the last to die. In the U.S.A. it was observed that the stresses of World War 2 brought to the surface feelings one would have thought long dead since they were all by this time U.S. citizens. In some cases well-taught elders showed how deeprooted and destructive were the fleshly nationalistic feelings involving German, Japanese, British, and Italians. Of course with the majority this was not so; indeed the night my native city was devastated by bombing from German and Italian planes I was guest in a German home and ministering in an Italian assembly, in both of which we had a wonderful time of christian fellowship. The other attitude to ethnic differences however certainly did exist and caused deep wounds to the testimony. It is also not all that long ago that brethren of one colour would not have been welcome in some congregations of another colour.

We should not be surprised at this when we read of the

tensions between Jews and Gentiles in the early church, or of the grumblings between Helenists and Hebrews in Acts 6 over supposed partiality in the distribution of relief funds from the church. James, whose epistle is considered to have been one of the earliest if not the earliest, gives strong hints of class distinctions among believers. He warns against toadying to upper-class folk (ch.2), or allowing envy to lead to strife (ch.3), while in ch.5 the rich are warned against arrogance and greedy dishonesty, and the poor are urged to patience without murmuring or grumbling. All such distinctions from whatever source, then or now, are a blatant denial of the doctrine of the cross. They are all of the flesh, however disguised, and the cross, properly understood and applied, means the crucifying of the flesh in all its aspects.

CHAPTER 8

The Cross in Philippians

IN ch.2 of this Epistle Christ is presented as the example and model for His people. It would appear that in this assembly at Philippi all was not well; though there is no hint of doctrinal error or church disorder, there was a serious lack of oneness of mind and loving harmony (2:2). There were murmurings and disputings (2:14) and Euodias and Syntyche were obviously at odds with each other (4:2). The attitude of mind showed itself in a striving for prominence and place. Each would appear to have been pushing for selfish advantage and looking after his own interests rather than those of the whole body.

The cure is brought before them in the words: "Let this mind be in you which was also in Christ Jesus who... humbled Himself and became obedient unto death, even the death of the cross". The words omitted here are extremely important but are not essential to our theme except perhaps for one point often missed and to which we refer.

In 2:6 the words, "thought it not robbery to be equal with God" are more accurately translated as "to be on an equality with God" (RV, JND, Alford, W.E. Vine *et al*). Vine is particularly helpful in his exposition of Philippians (vol.2 *Collected Writings*, p.469) where he quotes almost verbatim from E.H. Gifford's *The Incarnation*, giving full credit of course. "The whole point is that what Christ relinquished when He came forth from the Father was not equality with God which would refer to what He *was* in essence and inherently and therefore could not be relinquished without His ceasing to *be* God. It referred to position with the Father. In other words He left the position; He remained in essence what He eternally was."

That the passage is hortatory is clear, since Christ is held up to us as a model to be imitated in His ways of thinking; in His willingness to surrender a position which was rightly His; in taking the low place; and in thus becoming the obedient bondservant. Here the divine Son, in order to bring the full measure of devotion to the Father (as the first table of the law required), and the full measure of blessing to man (as the second table required), does exactly what the young man in Mark 10 shrank from doing, even while professing a desire to follow Christ. Our blessed Lord gave up His place in the glory for one poverty, He gave up His position of authority in humbling Himself to become a dependent man. He whom the universe obeyed became obedient in submission to the will of the Father; without limits or qualifications, even to the point of death on a cross, yet He never emptied Himself of His deity. In the writer's hearing C.F. Hogg once made the statement that deity was not something which Christ had, but essentially what He was, therefore if deity empties itself of deity it becomes nonentity.

To Christ this meant not only hardship, suffering, and loss but acceptance of the reproach of being rejected by His covenant people and even by those who owed their existence to Him. They were dependent on Him for their very life even while they were nailing Him to the cross. The path He voluntarily chose led not only to death, but the cross-death, where He was mocked, degraded, abused, and insulted. This is the way of life and the pattern of thinking laid before us to be followed, and it is seen in the chapter to be imitated by Paul, Timothy, and Ephaph-roditus. Paul is willing and even glad to be poured out for *them*. Timothy will care for *their* state with no thought for his own. Not regarding his own life Epaphroditus in service for *others* came near to death. Paul says of himself in 3:10 that he wants "to be made conformable unto His death", that is to die as Christ died, to be cut on the pattern of that death, to see self crucified. He also tells us his reason for wishing this, and it is that he "might attain unto resurrection from the dead". Paul was in no doubt as to his own future resurrection at the Lord's return. What he yearns for here in personal experience is to walk day by day in resurrection power as one crucified with Christ but now experiencing "the power of *his* resurrection.

The sources of trouble at Philippi have haunted the church from the beginning and we must recognise with shame that the same ugly characteristics of the flesh have brought division and spiritual sterility to many an assembly. There is no hint in the Philippian letter of unsound doctrine such as there was at Corinth or Galatia, yet the flesh was obviously active as we see from various warnings by the apostle. We too might glory in doctrinal soundness yet fail to deal with the activity of the flesh as referred to in the first paragraph of this chapter. There we noticed lack of oneness of heart, lack of loving harmony, murmurings, disputings, open quarrelling as in the case of Euodias and Syntyche. We are not free from the more subtle carnality seen in striving after vain glory (place, prominence, popularity), feelings of superiority, selfish pushing for personal advantage in looking after one's own interests rather than those of others. This all reeks of the flesh or, as it is called elsewhere, carnality. As we hold the mirror up to ourselves we should surely realise that there is need for confession and cleansing. Then would come the sharp medicine of the cross as we read on our knees from Gal 5:17, "The flesh lusteth against the Spirit and the Spirit against the flesh, and these are contrary one to the other". They that are Christ's have crucified the flesh with its affections and lusts (v.2). Finally, "God forbid that I should glory save in the cross of our Lord Jesus Christ by which the world is crucified unto me and I unto the world" (6:14).

It is worth noting here that the word translated "world" in this last verse is not the physical earth, nor the geographical inhabited world, nor as in some places this "age". It is the word *kosmos*; the attractive and organised world of society, business, politics, art, science of which the worldlings are so proud and which can become such a trap for the Christian if he is tempted to get into its competitive lifestyle.

CHAPTER 9

Results of Failing to Embrace the Teaching of the Cross

IN the six passages in the Synoptic Gospels where our Lord Himself expounded the doctrine of the cross we found that in every case failure to accept this cross would bring loss, the ruination of the life for God, and lack of reward at His coming. In Phil 3:17-19 it is our conviction that we are given a divinely-inspired outline of the results of evading the cross or fighting against its meaning in our own hearts. The whole portion merits more careful consideration than is usually given to it.

Some think that vv.18, 19 must be seen as applying to unbelievers but the whole surrounding context both preceding and following make this interpretation hard to defend.

From the beginning of the section at 3:1 believers are addressed, exhorted, and warned. Those in view are three times referred to as "brethren" (vv.1, 12, 17). Then in the whole middle portion of the chapter he speaks of himself as in a race in which, with his eye on the finishing line and the reward, he strains toward the mark. He readily admits that he has neither "attained" (to reach or arrive at) nor been "perfect" (to have finished or completed) in reference to the course. Then in v.15 associating himself with his readers (note the phrase "let us"), he presses the exhort-ation on those who are mature (AV "perfect") "to be thus minded" (to think in the way he has been describing). Unsaved people would never be referred to as "perfect" or "mature". Then in v.17 again comes the appeal marked as urgent by the opening word "brethren, be followers (imitators) of me and mark them that walk so as ye have us for an ensample". In more current English this would be: Keep your eye on those who walk after our example.

Then in vv.20, 21 to continue our examination in the succeeding context in order to stimulate them to the greatest effort and to demand of them the greatest sacrifices here on earth he turns their eyes heavenward from whence they looked for a Saviour, the Lord Jesus Christ. Then follows the marvellous uplifting cry that when that One comes we shall be changed, transformed, made like Himself.

Paul has put before them examples to keep in view and to follow, including four in ch 2. Now with grief he calls attention to others not as examples to be followed, but as examples of what not to follow. These have shrunk back from the high cost of true discipleship and have ended up in ruination and loss, exactly the words of the Gospels that we have considered. But we must examine vv.18, 19 carefully.

Those referred to must have been well known in Philippi for Paul says he has mentioned them often before. As he brings them up again he does so weeping. Would he have used unbelievers as a warning for believers? Would the fleshly way of life of unconverted people have caused grief? Surely He would not have expected anything else from them. But these of whom he speaks have wrung his heart with sadness by their walk. He calls them "enemies of *the cross* of Christ" – not enemies of Christ, as it is often mis-quoted, but opponents, those who set themselves against the teaching of the cross of Christ. They will resist it and its demands. They will even fight against it for themselves since they do not like this doctrine, and do not want to pay the high price of reproach, or face the rejection, the mockery of a world in which they would prefer to be more comfortable. What cause for tears it is to see those who have been willing to accept the sacrificial and sub-stitutionary *death* of Christ with all its blessings and benefits, but who shrink back from, or even perhaps oppose and struggle against the implications of the *cross* of Christ. Does Christ perhaps weep too?

Let us now look honestly at the Holy Spirit's analysis of the basic characteristics of those so described in the passage. In v.18 this course is given from God's viewpoint in four steps which begin with the end result and then trace backwards through the steps which led to that result. To follow the development of the downward path we must reverse this order and begin at what is last mentioned, the first steps, which led to the final ruin of the life.

1. Such people mind earthly things. Vine says that "to mind" is to set the mind on and adds "it implies moral interest or reflection, not mere unreasoning opinion". It is more, than something coming to or crossing one's mind, but means a deliberate fixing of the mind, or thinking constantly of something desired and aimed at. See Phil 1:27; 2:2; 2:5; compare also Rom 12:16, "Mind not high things" and 12:2 with "renewing of the mind". Those we are studying insist on setting their minds on their own personal interests which are connected with earth in contrast with those in previous verses who "looked for the Saviour from heaven". These people will not give up in the interest of others what they prize for themselves. They do not want to "make themselves of no reputation" or to be "poured out" for others as were Christ, Paul, Timothy, and Epaphroditus according to ch.2. Their minds are firmly set on the material interests of earth like Demas who abandoning Paul in prison "loved this present age, and departed..." (2 Tim 4:15). How different Paul who with many others had set the heart on "his appearing"! How unlike Epaphroditus also who stayed with Paul in prison and because of the work drove himself to the very brink of death!

   Step one in the downward path is the setting of the mind and heart toward earthly things for the satisfaction of

the self-life. That of course indicates a setting aside of
the cross and all it stands for.

2. Such people glory in their shame. At first sight one might
    wonder how anyone would or could glory in their own shame,
    but perhaps it might help if we saw it to mean that they were
    glorying in what they, as Christians, ought to have been
    ashamed of. The original word trans-lated as "shame" here
    is the same word as is translated "filthy (lucre)" in 1 Tim 3:3.
    This is usually explained as meaning "base (gain)" or gain
    that is unworthy of the character of one of following it. In 1
    Cor 2:7,8, Paul showed that worldly wisdom, in which so many
    gloried, led the leaders of the nation to commit the most
    disgusting and brutal act of folly the world has even witnessed.
    Yet they gloried in their shameful blunder.

    In the very chapter we are studying (Phil 3) we see that
    Saul of Tarsus thought he was doing God service and
    gloried in his religious zeal, persecuting the people of
    God! Once his eyes were turned to the Lord Jesus he
    saw his actions in their true light and called them "but
    dung and dross" of which he was now ashamed. In 1 Cor
    5 the carnal Christians there did not mourn over an
    incestuous adulterer sitting with them in the gathering
    but were "puffed up", preening themselves, glorying in
    what they should have been ashamed of. Again in 3 John
    the apostle speaks of Diotrephes who loves to have the
    preeminence; his usurpation was an odious act of pride.
    Not content with this or in any way ashamed of such
    actions he kept on "prating" against John, with
    apparently no sense of shame. It is therefore a sad thing
    when a believer gets so far away from the spirit of Christ
    that he becomes proud of his advancement in the very
    world which murdered his Master. He may be glorying
    in having "reached the top" and made himself a repu-
    tation in the world of business, science, art, or even
    politics and feel a glow of satisfaction and achievement.

If, however, it were all seen in the light of the cross, the sanctuary, and the Judgment Seat of Christ, the glorying might well turn to shame.

3. Such people's God is their belly. This is the next step and to us in our language it sounds harsh and physical. We miss the point here however, if we restrict the reference to the demands of appetite at the dinner table. Here, by the use of a well known literary figure of speech one organ – we would to-day say the stomach – is put for all appetites because it is the one which demands satisfaction so constantly and so insistently. The appetite for food is God-given and legitimate and, when intelli-gently controlled, cannot be condemned. To make a god of it, however, or any of the desires for which it here stands, is the beginning of trouble and even tragedy.

We must remember that there is such a thing as a hunger for power, position, material things or the money which would enable us to obtain them. There can also be a hunger for place, or prominence, which seems to have troubled some Philippian believers according to ch.2 of that letter to say nothing of popularity or of success. Our society to-day seems to dangle before the eyes of so many in the business world or the academic world these desires or appetites which means making all else bend to them and leads in turn to the putting all else of worth in second place or worse.

What a sad thing it is when a declared disciple of the Lord Jesus spends the greater part of his time working to satisfy his own ambitions and desires! He does this while professing to follow One who never had a desire apart from doing the will of him who sent Him, and who never allowed self to occupy His thoughts, much less to dominate His life. He came not to be served, but to serve; not to get but to give. He gave even His own life. His very food was to do the will of Him who sent Him and to finish his work. He "must needs go through Samaria", hungry, thirsty and weary to meet the needs of a sinful and degraded woman, who at least at first was not even gracious or grateful. But the professed disciple of the Philippian passage under study is, in all this, far from his Master's path and example in seeking the satisfaction of his own interests in a world which rejected that Master.

4. Such people's end is destruction. Some, having decided that those spoken of in these two verses are unconverted enemies of Christ find it an easy step to assume that the "destruction" referred to is the eternal destruction of the unrepentant in Hell and the Lake of Fire. While one might perhaps make an application of this in the gospel, as is done in the "what-shall-it-profit-a-man" passages of the Gospels, we believe it does not do justice to the text or serve as sound interpretation of this portion in Philippians. As we have said already, the sort of behaviour outlined here is what we would expect of worldlings who have nothing else to live for; Paul would hardly have been shocked to tears by bad behaviour in worldlings. It is something vastly different when seen in a child of God and a professed disciple of Christ.

First we must understand, as Vine points out, that the word translated "destruction" here can have the meaning, in noun and verb forms, not of loss of being but of well-being. As we have already seen in the Gospel passages considered, it is used of the wine skins that "perished" or were ruined for their original purpose, and of the "waste" attributed by Judas to Mary's act of worship. But most convincing of all is the fact that in the teaching on the cross in the Gospels, with which we are still dealing, the very root-word is used for the "loss" on one's life when it is saved for self: "He that saveth his life (in this world) will lose it, but he that loseth (same word) his life for my sake shall save (or have, or keep) it unto life eternal", or in Luke 9:25 where in the parallel passage the words are "lose himself or be cast away" which we saw is given by most authorities as "destroying (or ruining) himself and suffering loss" – a redeemed life ruined and lost for God.

A worthwhile study in this connection is 1 Tim 6:9 where the context surely has believers in mind. They are warned that "They that will be (are determined to be) rich fall into temptation and a snare, and into many hurtful lusts which drown men in destruction and perdition". We might accurately paraphrase this for better understanding as those determined to be rich fall into temptation and a snare (for an adversary is at work) and into foolish and unjurious desires or appetites (for self and the flesh are at work) which overwhelm men in ruination and loss. Both these last nouns are those found in the teaching of Christ on discipleship in Matthew, Mark, and Luke, as we have noted.

So we might summarise the teaching of this Philippian passage dealing with those who oppose the doctrine of the cross and its implications as:

1. Setting the mind on earthly and material things as the goal of life.

2. Glorying in what should be considered spiritually as shame.

3. Making personal appetites, desires, and objectives the god of our lives, commanding devotion to the point where they usurp the place of Christ in the hearts.

4. The ruination of the life redeemed by God for His own use, and the consequent loss to the individual at the Judgment Seat of Christ.

CHAPTER 10

Conditions for Discipleship Re-considered

TO gather up and summarise what we have been
considering on this subject it would be hard to find better
words than those of F.W. Grant on Matt 16 (*The Numerical
Bible*, published Loizeaux brothers, Neptune, N.J.). He
writes: "[Christ] shows the disciples that He must go to
Jerusalem and suffer many things of the elders, and the
chief priests, and scribes, and be killed and the third day
be raised up. It is not atonement of which He speaks, but
of rejection by men; the human side of His death, not the
divine... But the Lord not only declares His own death; He
announces it also as the path for all his followers... The
conditions for discipleship are laid down with the most
decisive plainness for all, without exception. It is a world
which had crucified Christ through which our path lies and
we have to make up our minds to face it. It is evident that
He does not hold out any hope of the world changing, nor
therefore of the path changing. We know how fully the
generation immediately following the days of Christ on
earth were tested. Can we fairly refuse the application to
ourselves to-day?... The Lord's words must have a present
application to us to-day if we are His disciples".

To this we would add the words of A.W. Tozer in his
pamphlet *The Old Cross and the New*. "The cross is a symbol
of death. It stands for the abrupt, violent end of a human
being. The man in Roman times who took up his cross and
started down the road had already said good-by to his
friends. He was not coming back. He was not going to have
his life redirected; he was going to have it ended. The cross
made no compromise, modified nothing, spared nothing; it
slew the man... God salvages the individual by liquidating him

and then raising him again in newness of life".

In the application of this to the individual we have seen that it operates in different contexts and none of the contexts encountered was foreign to our day. The lessons of those contexts are to be learned today. In Corinthians we have seen it applied to congregational or assembly behaviour, for in that local church all was marred by unjudged sin, specifically incestuous adultery. There was wrangling over personal rights to the point of taking a brother in the Lord before the pagan law courts, and that to their own public shame. The flesh showed itself also in the almost childish abuse of their spiritual gifts, one instance of which was in speaking to audiences in tongues which no one understood. Still another was the speaking of women in public meetings of the church when this was expressly forbidden. All this sprang from the self-centred activity of the flesh despite the apostles having taught clearly in Gal 5:24 that "They are Christ's have crucified the flesh with its passions and desires" (RV; JND). And in the late twentieth century when there is disorder, even public disorder in some assemblies there is a clamant need for the teaching of the cross.

In the churches of Galatia it was not the loose disorderliness of the flesh so much as the harsh narrowness of legalism, for the flesh will always run to extremes. True, in Galatia it flowed from a doctrinal position but the spirit which this generates, down to our own day, is often one of bigotry and a judgmental attitude which sometimes can lead perhaps without the realisation of it to an unbiblical sectarianism. May God deliver us from such a spirit as we apply cross truth to our lives.

In Philippians the problem seems to have been that of individuals striving for positions of superiority and vain glory. There were murmurings and disputings, as well as a tendency for each to be looking "after his own things", rather than the good of the whole congregation. In ch.4

two women were obviously in some sort of contention. All this is quite obviously the flesh or the "self" asserting itself. As crucified with Christ, in a practical sense there would be included in the Christian's duty to "mortify (put to death) the deeds of the body" (Rom 8:13) and "mortify" his members (Col 3:5). The wording here might seem strange – putting deeds to death or even one's member! but when we read the rest of the Colossian verse it makes the meaning clear by listing some of the activities or deeds of the members as "fornication, uncleanness... covetousness". These are urges and activities of our flesh which must be dealt the death blow; no quarter being given – they must go in the light of the cross.

In Hebrews the temptation is different but the theme is the same. They seemed in danger of "growing weary and fainting in their minds. So violent had become the sufferings and persecutions, and so persistent the opposition and the pressures upon them to conform that they seemed almost ready to give up, shrink back from it all, and look for an easier way. Then comes the Holy Spirit's rallying cry, "consider Him who endured such contradiction of sinners against Himself" and, "run with patience (same word as 'endurance') the race that is set before us, looking unto Jesus who... endured *the cross* despising the shame, and is set down at the right hand of God".

In recognising the need of endurance, let us not give up or retreat into selfish living. We sing about these truths in the words:

> We lose what on ourselves we spend.
> We have as treasure without end,
> Whatever, Lord, to Thee we lend
> Who giveth all.

The question is as to how much we mean what we are singing. It has been said that it is as easy to sing a lie as to tell a lie. Perhaps as never before there is a need for the grace of continuance. The evidence of endurance is not easily provided but the fortitude which perseveres can be resourced by the same Christ and will be rewarded by the same God as the Hebrews knew but only if at the cross are judged the fleshly desires after ease and effortless painless Christianity.

May our prayer be framed in the light of the true meaning of the cross, "Lord, teach us to learn what Christ taught about His cross and to think as Christ thought as He faced the cross".